Introduction

Almost daily, I meet tales of people with incredible heartache, tragedy, or misfortune. Others feel worn down by life's normal stresses and strains. No matter what life is handing you right now, Lent is here to remind you to hang on to hope and turn to Jesus. He's walking the path beside you.

Hope is what we all need to make it through life. Hope is there to remind you that you're never alone—Jesus is always there with you, pushing, pulling, encouraging, loving, and carrying you through.

During this Lent, I encourage you to reach out to Jesus. Listen as Jesus comforts your heart and says, "I know it hurts. I'm not giving up on you." Try to respond when he challenges you to change a self-destructive behavior or habit that sabotages your relationships. And always look for the persons Jesus sends to care for you. They understand what you're going through because they've had their own setbacks. And they've bounced back. They'll pick you up, walk with you, listen, and welcome your tears.

Use these practical reflections, with down-to-earth suggestions, to learn how to live more fully in Jesus and to live in hope. Squeeze all you can out of these pages. My prayer is that, when Easter arrives, you will feel refreshed, rejuvenated, hopeful, and ready to help Jesus bring hope and healing to all the hurting hearts around you.

TWENTY-THIRD PUBLICATIONS A division of Bayard
One Montauk Avenue, Suite 200; New London, CT 06320
(860) 437-3012 or (800) 321-0411; www.twentythirdpublications.com

Cover image: ©Sweetie1984 | Dreamstime

ISBN: 978-1-62785-335-4

Copyright ©2018 Joseph F. Sica. All rights reserved. No part of this publication may be reproduced in any manner without prior written permission of the publisher. Write to the Permissions Editor.

Printed in the U.S.A.

FEBRUARY 14 ■ *Ash Wednesday*

JOEL 2:12–18 » 2 CORINTHIANS 5:20—6:2 » MATTHEW 6:1–6, 16–18

Being a designated survivor

"Your Father who sees in secret will repay you." » MATTHEW 6:4

It's the night of the president's State of the Union Address when a devastating attack on the U.S. Capitol occurs. Tom Kirkman, the Secretary of Housing and Urban Development, is suddenly the designated survivor and becomes President of the United States. Thrust into his new position, Kirkman struggles to keep the country from dissolving into chaos.

Of course, this is the fictional basis of the ABC show *Designated Survivor*. But therein lies a lesson. Sometimes life blindsides us and we feel completely overwhelmed—a painful illness, a career setback, financial stress, betrayal, or sudden death. Life explodes, rocking our world.

When the unexpected occurs, give yourself a time-out. Catch your breath as you ponder what happened; then adjust. Ask, "What am I going to do now?" Then release your hurt into God's lap and lean on Jesus. Because the truth is, you need help. Pay attention as someone calls you out of the blue or shows up and walks alongside you. We must do what we can. It's up to God to do the rest. Trust God.

TO DO: Whom do you run to when the bottom drops out of your life? Create your "safe haven list." Include the people you can cry with as they hold you and listen, saying, "I understand. I've been there too."

TO PRAY: *Dear Lord, never let me miss an opportunity to help a friend whose world has crumbled under the weight of bad news. Amen.*

FEBRUARY 15 ■ *Thursday after Ash Wednesday*

DEUTERONOMY 30:15–20 » LUKE 9:22–25

Living unselfishly

"Take up your cross and follow me." » LUKE 9:23

"Well it's just my cross to bear," we say while going through illness, disaster, or misery of some kind. We may live with a difficult spouse, work with a cantankerous colleague, grieve a rebellious child, discover nasty rumors about ourselves, or disagree with someone politically, practically, or fundamentally. "It's just my cross to bear."

The cross Jesus asks us to carry involves living in a world unselfishly where other's needs are our priority. Lent is a great time to put those needs ahead of our own, starting at home. Read to your child; do the dishes without being asked; play a game with the family; watch a movie together and then talk about it. Reach out to others by visiting a lonely neighbor or someone in a nursing home or hospital.

Those spontaneous acts of caring and comfort can go a long way in easing a burden. A cooked meal, an afternoon chat, an errand run, a gentle hug, a personal note, a phone call—any of these can mean the world to someone in pain.

Living unselfishly means eliminating excuses for not getting involved. This Lent, choose to give up excuses and take action. There are people waiting for you.

TO DO: When your life is ending, you won't remember the moments of success, but rather the moments of filling needs and healing hurts. Reach out. It matters.

TO PRAY: *Dear Lord, regardless of how small my role, help me do my part toward easing someone's pain. Amen.*

FEBRUARY 16 — *Friday after Ash Wednesday*
ISAIAH 58:1–9A » MATTHEW 9:14–15

Joyology

"The days will come when the bridegroom is taken away from them." » MATTHEW 9:15

"What gets you through it?" I ask, acknowledging someone's deep pain. "Splashes of joy," they respond, refreshed and ready to keep going.

This is the key to the way we should live—simply and completely. Grounded in God as the foundation of all our joy, we align our actions, interactions, choices, and behaviors with a joyous *attitude* and *gratitude*. We can become joyologists.

Attitude. Things often don't go according to plan. Sometimes they go utterly and spectacularly wrong. Joyologists aren't free of life's speed bumps. Life even delivers them a truckload of lemons on occasion. But joyologists simply edit out the negative, recognizing that negativity breeds negativity. Then they edit in the good that is happening, no matter how little or much.

Gratitude. Joyologists don't worry obsessively, lament over the might-have-beens, or get caught up in "someday…." They are grateful for every moment, give thanks for the good in their lives, and appreciate the little things—a breathtaking sunset, an engaging conversation, a delicious meal. Fully engaged in the now, when life gets bumpy, they choose to power ahead.

God directs joyologists to connect with people who are having a hard time bouncing back, helping them turn the lemons into a refreshing glass of lemonade.

TO DO: If you're feeling lost and unsure, list the things in life that bring you joy and happiness. Then go and enjoy them.

TO PRAY: *Dear Lord, use me to spread joy and make my joy complete. Amen.*

FEBRUARY 17 • *Saturday after Ash Wednesday*

ISAIAH 58:9B–14 » LUKE 5:27–32

Demonstrating love

"Why do you eat and drink with tax collectors and sinners?" » LUKE 5:30

Troy Maxon (in the film *Fences*) tells his son Cory, "Don't you try and go through life worrying about if somebody like you or not. You best be making sure they doing right by you." Justifying this, he rants a litany of his struggles, telling Cory how happy he should be to have a home and food, albeit absent love and affection.

Saying "I love you" is the simplest, most no-frills way of keeping the parent/child attachment strong. So when you remind your children, "No texting at the table," or tell them they're not allowed to go to their friend's house unchaperoned, they will know it's coming from a place of love. It's not that you wish to inflict pain on them; rather, you're looking out for them. With love, they get it.

Character, responsibility, and doing the right thing can be taught while still demonstrating love. Sit down and talk with your kids. Show an interest in their lives. Hug them when they succeed, but even more when they fail. There are better ways to parent than Troy Maxon's way.

TO DO: When your children talk to you, put aside whatever you're doing and look them directly in the eyes. Let them know they're valuable. Schedule an electronics fast and do fun things together. Besides saying the words, let your gestures communicate your love for your children.

TO PRAY: *Dear Lord, help me to remember that children will not remember the material stuff, but they will remember the feeling of being cherished. Amen.*

FEBRUARY 18 ▪ *First Sunday of Lent*

GENESIS 9:8–15 » 1 PETER 3:18–22 » MARK 1:12–15

Fortified boundaries

He remained in the desert for forty days, tempted by Satan.
» MARK 1:13

"Touring isn't something I'm good at," Adele told the crowd at Auckland's Mt. Smart Stadium. "I don't know if I will ever tour again."

Boundaries are created when we understand and know what our personal limits are. When we try to do everything, we crash. Ultimately, we're stressed, pressed, sad, impatient, tired, and even angry; we feel weak and ashamed. To avoid going over the edge, we must recognize our boundaries and make the world comfortable for ourselves—while striving to be our absolute best within our comfort zone. Knowing our boundaries means downsizing, making healthy choices, or saying, "No, I can't do it."

We must also set healthy boundaries in our relationships by standing up for ourselves and refusing to tolerate pushy people or rude comments. Fortified boundaries preserve our integrity as we take responsibility for who we are by letting others know we have self-respect and won't tolerate having someone else define us. We are in the driver's seat of our lives.

Jesus just came from his desert duel with the devil, but Jesus stood his ground. By setting boundaries, he rendered the devil powerless.

TO DO: This Lent, give yourself permission to put you first. Choose a "Me Day." Go to a coffee shop, order a latte, and read a novel uninterrupted. Or come up with something uniquely you.

TO PRAY: *Dear Lord, sometimes I go over the limit for others and I feel drained. Encourage me to claim time for myself. Amen.*

FEBRUARY 19 ◾ *Monday of the First Week*

LEVITICUS 19:1–2, 11–18 » MATTHEW 25:31–46

Seeking the wounded

"Lord, when did we see you hungry or thirsty, or a stranger, or naked, or sick, or in prison, and didn't take care of you?" » MATTHEW 25:44

There are hurting people all around us. How many times have we passed by someone who is suffering without noticing them? Christian love defines how we respond to seeing the unseen in life. During Lent, we can enter their world, see their pain, and extend compassion.

It's our discomfort that has us offering our unsolicited advice or ignoring someone's feelings. "What you should do is…" "It's not that bad." "Oh, I've been through this myself before," we say as we share our own pain. Worst of all, our impatience prompts us to say, "Isn't it time you get over this?"

When the hurting invite us into their suffering, they aren't asking us to remove their pain. Healing is found when they meet others willing to enter that space together with them. They need to hear only eight words: I recognize your pain; I'm here with you. When someone says, "Ouch! That must really hurt," "I'm here," or "I care," they have room to express their emotions.

Be a seeker of hurting persons. You're needed more than you know. And when you find yourself in need, they'll find you. I guarantee they're there.

TO DO: Do you know someone struggling with life's hurts? Make it a point to connect with them and recognize their pain. You can change their life.

TO PRAY: *Dear Lord, some days feel too hard. But knowing someone cares eases my pain. Thanks for placing them in my life. Amen.*

FEBRUARY 20 ▪ *Tuesday of the First Week*

ISAIAH 55:10–11 » MATTHEW 6:7–15

Forgiving the debt

"If you forgive others their transgressions, your heavenly Father will forgive you."
» MATTHEW 6:14

A conversation can escalate into a full-scale argument, complete with underlying issues surfacing and participants landing in a bad place. Tones of voice change, critical comments appear, accusations fly. The warp-speed argument becomes a contest of who can win, so they bring in ammunition of comparisons and threats to support their position. Finally, they vow never to speak to each other again.

Family and friends, once warm and close, are now cold and distant, looking for ways to build higher walls. But the healthy choice dictates that we check our egos at the door and create means for reconciliation. Offer a kind word. A warm handshake. A simple question: "How's it going?" But no one wants to make that first step, which is the biggest obstacle in the strained relationship. Until someone budges and moves toward reconciliation, lives will be fraught with anger, bitterness, resentment, hatred, and revenge.

Each of us has been hurt by someone. It may have been years ago. Or yesterday. Big. Or little. It's up to each of us to decide: enough! It's gone on too long. Healing is needed. It's time.

TO DO: Our connection to people who have violated our trust or betrayed or abused us is lost. We can decide to make it permanent or move toward reconciliation. Look over your hurt list and see where you might be able to work on tearing down the walls and reuniting.

TO PRAY: *Dear Lord, push me to make the first move toward healing those wounded relationships. Amen.*

FEBRUARY 21 ■ *Wednesday of the First Week*

JONAH 3:1–10 » LUKE 11:29–32

In the blink of an eye

"At the preaching of Jonah they repented, and there is something greater than Jonah here." » LUKE 11:32

Thirty years ago, recording group Cinderella said, "Don't know what you got till it's gone." Foolishly, we assume that what we need will always be there. Writer Ashley Fern says, "Truth is, you knew what you had, you just never thought you'd lose it." We take it for granted, don't we?

We wake up one morning shocked when we've lost someone or something. We realize how grateful we should have been in the first place. Life is about cherishing and celebrating the people and opportunities we have now—friendships, health, employment, education, home, success, and the plain old everyday things.

But tragedy can strike in the blink of an eye; often it does. A single moment alters everything. It's a wake-up call to realize how quickly it could all be gone. We must always be vigilant and fully participating in life and relationships.

Don't let your life be a collection of what's lost because you didn't pay attention. No matter how much you'd love to have something back, once it's gone, it's gone. Since do-overs in life are rare, treasure all you have and consciously enjoy every moment.

TO DO: Life can change quickly. It's time to take an inventory of all we have that is precious to us. Be grateful and mindful of it.

TO PRAY: *Dear Lord, it's too late to cry over what we have lost and wish we'd have it back. Keep our eyes focused on all we have. Amen.*

FEBRUARY 22 ■ *Thursday of the First Week*

1 PETER 5:1–4   »   MATTHEW 16:13–19

One wounded soul at a time

"And I tell you, you are Peter, and on this rock I will build my church." » MATTHEW 16:18

In an interview with the Jesuit magazine *La Civiltà Cattolica*, Pope Francis said, "The thing the church needs most today is the ability to heal wounds and to warm the hearts of the faithful. The church needs to be a field hospital after battle."

When people's lives are wounded or broken, they need soothing healing, not harsh judgment. For Lent, let's not only go to church; let's *be* the church. Let's do what Jesus did—go to where the lost are and love them into the kingdom of God. Jesus invited tax collectors, prostitutes, thieves, and run-of-the-mill sinners into his circle of love and healing.

Search out just one person who has taken a sabbatical from the church. Listen to their story. Is their soul wounded? Is there deep pain? Is there emotional or spiritual suffering?

What they need is a welcoming community to walk alongside of them and offer healing. Invite them to bring their hurts to church; then be patient with them A physical injury takes time to heal; spiritual pains need time as well. But knowing they have a committed care-connection with a loving community brings healing.

TO DO: People's injuries are real. They need caring friends as they heal. Use the remaining time of this season to invite just one person who is hurting to come to church.

TO PRAY: *Dear Lord, you went out of your way to feel others' pain and brought healing through your gentle words and actions. Help me do the same. Amen.*

FEBRUARY 23 ▪ *Friday of the First Week*

EZEKIEL 18:21-28 » MATTHEW 5:20-26

No vacancy

"Settle with your opponent quickly." » MATTHEW 5:25

Renting space in our heads to people and situations is a common epidemic that often causes us worry and stress. All the stuff they bring impacts the way we feel. A comment from the past, a nasty action, a personal failure—we simply can't shake it loose.

We end up hurting ourselves more than the actual events did because we allow the scenarios to camp out in our heads. As we try to convince ourselves we're in the right, we act out conversations we wish we'd had. When we find ourselves slipping into the rehashing fests, it's time to step back and talk back.

Step back and realize the people we have allowed to reside in our heads are most likely unaware of it. Next, talk back to yourself and say, "Stop it!" Then evict them and move on with a clear head, filled with peace and happiness.

Once we kick them out, we'll have space available to rent to people who love us and enable us to grow—the people who make us smile and laugh. Life is much too short to waste it otherwise.

TO DO: When you put up a "For Rent" sign, lease to those who will encourage and empower you. To anyone else, the space is unavailable.

TO PRAY: *Dear Lord, give me the wisdom to know whom to allow into my head and the courage to ask them to leave when they are hurting me. Amen.*

FEBRUARY 24 ▪ *Saturday of the First Week*
DEUTERONOMY 26:16–19 » MATTHEW 5:43–48

Starving our worries

"So be perfect, just as your heavenly Father is perfect." » MATTHEW 5:48

Wrapping up the tour of a creepy old castle, the guide asks a young woman how she enjoyed it. She admits to being a bit worried about seeing a ghost in some of the dark cobwebbed rooms and passages.

"Don't worry," says the guide. "I've never seen a ghost all the time I've been here."

"How long is that?" asks the girl.

"About three hundred years."

Worry—it's been called the universal addiction. Worrying about what we're going to eat, how we're going to pay the bills, what's going on with the kids, the job, what we heard on the news…just constant worry.

Worry, however, is not the same as healthy concern. It's natural to be concerned about an interview or a medical test. But when it preoccupies our every moment, it's no longer concern—it's worry. It's all consuming and debilitating, and it steals quality time from people we can enjoy or things we like to do.

No one's immune. But we can stop feeding our worry. Identify your worry and starve it over time.

TO DO: Use the Scarlett O'Hara method. When the southern belle was in distress, she never let worry get her down. She said, "I'll think about that tomorrow." Put your worries off, and chances are you'll forget them.

TO PRAY: *Dear Lord, worry can keep me up all night; but trusting in you can give me a peaceful sleep. Amen.*

FEBRUARY 25 • *Second Sunday of Lent*

GENESIS 22:1–2, 9A, 10–13, 15–18 » ROMANS 8:31B–34 » MARK 9:2–10

It's pivotal

"Rabbi, it is good that we are here!" » MARK 9:5

A promotion, a wedding, or the start of a family—how exciting! An accident, a terminal illness, the news that someone we love is dying—how terrible! It's the latter type of news that throws us for a loop. We go through the motions, haunted by events, our lives forever altered.

Looking back on my life, I can pinpoint several of those moments—firsthand tragedies that changed me or tragedies I, as a priest, shared with others. I've learned it doesn't matter what pivotal moment comes our way; our response determines whether it will make us or break us.

Since everything is in turmoil, it's necessary to take baby steps. You need to be able to wrap your head around it and ask, "What just happened?" Then go to God. Have a heart-to-heart with him. Share your feelings, ask him for guidance, and listen as he responds. Do your part by pitching in and using your inner strengths. They helped you get through tough times before and they will help you again, even if this situation seems more difficult. Tackling it together with God, you'll have the power to pull through. Don't let a setback discourage you. Just try again.

TO DO: List your pivotal moments. Then write the ways they have changed who you are.

TO PRAY: *Dear Lord, guide me with your wisdom and strength to get through the pivotal experiences I will face. Amen.*

FEBRUARY 26 ■ *Monday of the Second Week*

DANIEL 9:4B–10 » LUKE 6:36–38

STALL snap judgments

"Do not judge and you will not be judged." » LUKE 6:37

"What does she see in him?" Based on one small thing—someone's weight, their hair, their vocabulary, their accent—we sum up a person, forming snap judgments without even knowing the person. Little to no effort is made to get acquainted or to see whether our initial impression is accurate.

Once you make up your mind about someone, it's difficult to change it. Our judgment often causes that person to react in the same way we are judging them. What's the antidote? STALL.

Stop judging. Be mindful of your thoughts. Notice when a judgment is forming, and stop it.

Try walking in their shoes. Converse with them in order to gain an understanding of the circumstances in their life.

Accept them. Once you understand, accept that person for who they are—without trying to change them.

Love them. Even if you don't know them or hated them in the past, love them as a sister or brother, no matter who they are.

Let God be the judge. God sees the whole picture. We don't.

Are you up for a challenge? Go for a day, then a week, making judgment-free living part of your routine. Remember: by judging the oyster and dismissing it, we may miss the pearl. Same goes with those we judge.

TO DO: Do something special for someone who has been inaccurately judged and dismissed.

TO PRAY: *Dear Lord, forgive me for the times I quickly judge others before hearing their story. Amen.*

FEBRUARY 27 ■ *Tuesday of the Second Week*
ISAIAH 1:10, 16–20 » MATTHEW 23:1–12

Did I just say that?

"For they preach but they do not practice." » MATTHEW 23:3

"Sticks and stones may break my bones, but words will never hurt me." Have you ever used this playground tactic as a comeback after someone belittled you? The problem is, sarcasm, insults, accusations, and name-calling all have the power to cut us deeply.

We recklessly put what we're thinking into words, with no concern about how our words will harm another person. The wrong thing said at the wrong time causes others' defenses to flare. Barriers follow. The end result? Damaged relationships.

Think about the words that have deflated you: "You can't do anything right." "You're ugly." "You're stupid." You felt you simply weren't good enough, right? The words crushed your spirit. On the other hand, think about the words that have inflated you. "You're so talented!" "I'm proud of you!" "I knew you could do it." These soft and encouraging words expressed concern and care, love and forgiveness. They built you up and made you feel valuable.

Be responsible with your words; you use them all day, every day. Choose them wisely and carefully, remembering that they will stay with a person for quite a while—encouraging or discouraging them for years.

TO DO: Select a mealtime every week where everyone in the family will say something encouraging about every other person. Then end with a prayer.

TO PRAY: *Dear Lord, when my words are derogatory, remind me that you say: "I have created no human person by that description." Amen.*

FEBRUARY 28 ▪ *Wednesday of the Second Week*
JEREMIAH 18:18–20 » MATTHEW 20:17–28

Enough about you!

"But those who exalt themselves will be humbled, and those who humble themselves will be exalted." » MATTHEW 23:12

Ann's friend Cathy was driving her crazy, constantly talking about herself, expecting center stage all the time. All-about-me people are tough. Most of us fall into this category occasionally. But those who take it to the extreme have a "holier than thou" attitude coupled with a need to always be right and have the last word.

Whether at work or in our families, we're all acquainted with people like Cathy. Demanding one-sided attention, they want listening ears, empathy, and agreement. Because they are not even aware of their behavior, their chances of changing are slim.

So how do we manage them? There's no point in going back and forth with someone who feels they're the center of the universe. They'll just get the best of you. It's important that you stand up for yourself and not stoop to their level. The battle simply isn't worth fighting. Distance yourself from them and, rather, connect with healthy and positive people not in need of the spotlight.

TO DO: Be civil to the Cathys in your life—bring up your own interests without letting them hijack the conversation. They'll disengage once they realize you're not going to give them the attention they crave.

TO PRAY: *Dear Lord, it's never just about me. Help me respect others' needs, feelings, dreams, and faith. Amen.*

MARCH 1 ■ *Thursday of the Second Week*
JEREMIAH 17:5–10 » LUKE 16:19–31

Small things forgotten

"Remember that during your lifetime you had everything you wanted, and Lazarus had nothing." » LUKE 16:25

Our genuine, authentic selves hide in the small things we've forgotten. The big moments—graduation, marriage, babies, first home, dream job—are just highlights of our personal stories. The tale is written in the ordinary and common moments—the unconsidered, unnoticed, and unwanted. This is where we find love, peace, happiness, and God, making life absolutely worthwhile.

Take a break. Give yourself a day to rediscover the significant moments that have shaped your life. Find a quiet place to sit, power-down the laptop, silence the cellphone and other distractions. Rediscover the people, events, books, movies, photos, comforts, and music that have touched your life—the small things that, when recalled, have significance.

Moonlight Graham, magically brought to life by Burt Lancaster in the 1989 film *Field of Dreams*, muses about his only day as a big league player: "You know, we just don't recognize the most significant moments of our lives while they're happening. Back then I thought, 'Well, there'll be other days.' I didn't realize that that was the only day." Take time to discover and cherish the small things forgotten.

TO DO: What small things are you taking with you from the life you're living right now? Carefully select one today and appreciate it.

TO PRAY: *Dear Lord, keep my eyes open to all the significant possibilities right under my nose. Amen.*

MARCH 2 ■ *Friday of the Second Week*
GENESIS 37:3–4, 12–13A, 17B–28A » MATTHEW 21:33–43, 45–46

The green-eyed monster

"This is the heir. Come, let us kill him and acquire his inheritance." » MATTHEW 21:38

Patricia sarcastically belittles people who are more attractive than she, diminishes their accomplishments, and delights in their struggles or failures. Why? Because she's envious of those whose lives seem better than hers.

The green-eyed monster can be a friend or a foe. As a friend, envy can motivate us to improve our lives by working harder. Someone else's success can push us to set healthy goals or to change direction in our career. As a foe, it's fueled by a desire to have everything our neighbors have and more. We feel we've been shortchanged in life and what we have is never good enough. After all, don't we deserve what they have? Resentment kicks in, camouflaged by a fake smile for the benefit of others.

When you wallow in envy, you discount what you have. So, what do you do when this foe is gaining a foothold? Wrestle with the green-eyed monster and tame it by focusing on your own backyard. Resist taking inventory of your neighbor's stuff—the in-ground swimming pool, the luxury car, the nice lawn furniture. Rather than fixating on what you don't have, stop, look, and cherish what you do have—your intrinsic worth, love, family, friends, and more.

TO DO: Volunteer at a homeless shelter or soup kitchen and use this experience as an opportunity to take stock of all you have rather than what you're lacking.

TO PRAY: *Dear Lord, train my eyes to look only in my own backyard without peeking into the neighbor's yard. Amen.*

MARCH 3 ■ *Saturday of the Second Week*

MICAH 7:14–15, 18–20 » LUKE 15:1–3, 11–32

SAW the anger

Then he became angry and refused to go in. » LUKE 15:28

The quote "Anger is one letter short of danger" is attributed to various people. But the meaning is universal. As anger boils within us, we lash out, eventually erupting. Bad things happen, lives are damaged, wounds are inflicted, and relationships are shattered. A moment of anger can destroy what it took a lifetime to build.

Here's how to avoid knee-jerk reactions and safely rein in our raging bull—SAW:

Sense what is happening. As your blood pressure rises, face reddens, irritation increases, and fists clench, step back and cool down before the anger erupts. Avoid saying or doing something you'll regret by saying, "This conversation is upsetting me. I need time to think about it."

Aware. As anger boils, be aware of the people, places, and things that make you heated. Give them a name—relationship disputes, mistreatment, feeling used, lies, interrupted plans, inequity.

Work to solve the problem by addressing what sparked it. Vent your feelings. Talk with someone. Pray about it.

Life is packed with frustrating moments. Harsh words are exchanged, feelings are hurt, and tempers flare. We can't always control the circumstances, but we can control our reactions.

TO DO: When you're ready to explode, repeat a calming phrase: "Take it easy." Listen to music, write in a journal, sip some tea—whatever it takes to help you cool down.

TO PRAY: *Dear Lord, before I snap, I'll say your name to calm me and protect my relationships. Amen.*

MARCH 4 — *Third Sunday of Lent*

EXODUS 20:1–25 » 1 CORINTHIANS 1:22–25 » JOHN 2:13–25
OR, FOR YEAR A: EXODUS 17:3–7 » ROMANS 5:1–2, 5–8 » JOHN 4:5–42

No, no, no!

Jesus, knew them all, and didn't need anyone to testify about human nature.
» JOHN 2:24–25

Unable to say "no" and walk away, Susan is a borderline doormat—a "people pleaser." She worries about what others think, need, and want, but rarely asks anyone for anything in return.

Equipped with a need to be emotional caretakers, people pleasers say "yes" out of habit. Can you identify? Your sister asks you to babysit again this weekend. "Sure, I can do it," you reply, canceling your plans to have dinner with a friend.

All of us need healthy amounts of approval; but when it dominates our lives, it raises red flags. We become a mere collection of others' expectations. Begin this week by reducing the tendency to please others. Change the "yes" to "no." Remember, the first "no" is the hardest. Say it aloud and often, just so you can hear it come out of your mouth. Rehearse it. "No, I can't do that." Start with a simple "no" at first; then advance to more difficult situations. Don't offer explanations or give them opportunities for manipulation.

People will still like you and you won't be ostracized from the group just because your "yes" turns into "no." Unless, of course, they were using you anyway. In that case, you're better off without them.

TO DO: Write "No, No, No" on sticky notes and paste them on your mirrors, dashboard, and computer screen.

TO PRAY: *Dear Lord, when I'm putting myself last, give me the courage to say "no" and stick to it. Amen.*

MARCH 5 ■ *Monday of the Third Week*

2 KINGS 5:1–15B OR EXODUS 17:1–7 » LUKE 4:24–30 OR JOHN 4:5–42

Who asked you?

"It is no longer because of what you said that we believe, for we have heard for ourselves." » JOHN 4:42

Devastated, Julie could hardly sleep after hearing that her best friend's marriage was in jeopardy. A few days later, she saw her friend and asked, "How are things going?"

"Oh that?" her friend replied. "It was just a misunderstanding. We worked it out."

Julie couldn't believe the energy she had wasted on a problem that wasn't even hers. Putting our nose where it doesn't belong and interfering with situations that are none of our business can harm our relationships and wreak havoc on our health.

Meddling in other people's business, we think we have the solution because we know better than they do. But we can't always fix things for them. When someone you know encounters a struggle, rather than running to their rescue, give them the space and freedom to discover their own ways of dealing with life's ups and downs. Be there for them, but don't offer to make things right.

Jesus walked into the life of the Samaritan woman whose life was a shipwreck. He didn't offer a quick fix solution. Neither should we.

TO DO: When someone brings a problem to you, resist the temptation to fix it. Place a rubber band on your wrist and when you feel the need to offer advice, snap it, so you don't.

TO PRAY: *Dear Lord, when I find myself putting my nose where it doesn't belong, help me pull back before I ruin a good relationship. Amen.*

MARCH 6 ■ *Tuesday of the Third Week*

DANIEL 3:25, 34–43 » MATTHEW 18:21–35

Take my hand

And the lord of that slave felt compassion and released him. » MATTHEW 18:27

We all know someone who's experiencing loss through death, divorce, or relocation; someone who's received a dire diagnosis or is facing bitter disappointment; or someone feeling unappreciated, worried about job security, or thinking they're a failure. Many suffer in silence, believing no one understands what they're going through.

While it's easy for us to run and hide from someone who's hurting, we need to share their pain and offer a shoulder to lean on. Later, they might not remember your words, but they'll remember that you showed up, held their hand, and cried with them. Knowing they have a lifeline and are not facing their struggles alone makes life more bearable for them. Even though you can't fix their problems, you can offer your presence and concern.

Empathetic people connect easily because they've been in the same boat as those who are hurting. They speak loudly through their presence: "I'm standing with you… I'm hurting with you. Take my hand. We'll make it together."

Just knowing that someone will drop everything and be there with their undivided attention helps ease the burden of hard times. Compassionate care is costly, but real friends are willing to pay the price.

TO DO: Write a thank-you card and send it to someone who stood by you when everyone else walked away.

TO PRAY: *Dear Lord, help me to take my eyes off myself in order to connect with a person who is crying out for help. Amen.*

MARCH 7 ■ *Wednesday of the Third Week*
DEUTERONOMY 4:1, 5–9 » MATTHEW 5:17–19

Being TACTful

"I tell you the truth." » MATTHEW 5:18

Relationship counselor, the late John Gray, encouraged others to practice TACT when stating their needs, sharing their story, or expressing their feelings. TACT (*T*elling the *A*bsolute *C*omplete *T*ruth) requires that we come clean with each other, holding nothing back, without being disrespectful, hurtful, or rude.

A police officer stops you and asks, "Do you know how fast you were going?" You respond, "I didn't realize I was speeding." Your spouse asks, "Did you make that phone call?" You explain, "I tried, but it keeps going to voicemail." The boss praises you for work you didn't do. You bask in the compliments and say nothing. In a world of little white lies, half-truths, embellished experiences, and shaded realities, it's refreshing to find someone who tells it like it is.

We've all been there—sidestepping the truth in order to keep peace, escape consequences, get ahead, or make ourselves look better. If we lie, the consequences can be far more destructive and painful than the original conflict we tried to avoid. Our lives should be models of integrity. After all, for the Christian, honesty isn't just the best policy; it's the only policy.

TO DO: Say what you mean, and mean what you say. Keep practicing this until you have it mastered. It's the only way to be a reliable truth teller.

TO PRAY: *Dear Lord, I've said things that weren't really in my heart but sounded good. Forgive me. From now on, it's just the truth. Amen.*

MARCH 8 ■ *Thursday of the Third Week*

JEREMIAH 7:23–28 » LUKE 11:14–23

It's all about the TLC

"Every kingdom divided against itself becomes a desert."
» LUKE 11:17

If we're not careful, seemingly petty annoyances can erupt into an all-out war. Dirty clothes on the floor instead of in the hamper. A dinner date with our face buried in our phone. Self-centered channel surfing. Compliments unspoken. When we sweep inconsiderate behavior under the rug, it grows into an almost insurmountable mountain. That's when we need to call a truce and settle it with TLC.

Talking (I need). Have an eye-to-eye conversation. Turn off all electronic devices and focus on each other. Forget the tug-of-war of who's right or who's wrong. Put the issue on the table and speak truth, regardless of how much it hurts.

Listening (I understand). Avoid snappy comebacks. Try to see the world through the other person's eyes, essentially saying, "I want to understand you, where you're coming from, and why you do what you do." Move toward a resolution you can both live with.

Caring (I love). Despite the size of the problem, when you react with appreciation, you say to your loved one, "Your needs, happiness, and growth are important to me."

Once the problem is put to rest, commit to banning it from your relationship forever.

TO DO: When the TLC approach veers off course, circle back and try again. It's leading you into new emotional ground as you speak from your heart and work toward a solution together.

TO PRAY: *Dear Lord, keep pushing me to work on issues with patience and persistence. Amen.*

MARCH 9 ▪ *Friday of the Third Week*

HOSEA 14:2–10 » MARK 12:28–34

Falling in love...with me!

"The second commandment is this: You shall love your neighbor as yourself."
» MARK 12:31

"Why didn't you become you?" God asks in Elie Wiesel's *Souls on Fire*. God has gifted us with this incredible uniqueness and it's our responsibility to embrace it. Every person is different and has something to give that is unlike the gift of anyone else in the world. That alone should motivate us to love ourselves.

Choose to be satisfied and comfortable with yourself by liking who you are, appreciating and respecting the magnificence of you. Love the whole package, complete with the flaws, embarrassments, and quirkiness, along with all the wonderful qualities that make you one of a kind. Accepting, embracing, and loving yourself improves your days, relationships, work, leisure, faith, and future.

Just make sure there are no strings attached. It's not about when you get your dream job, lose fifteen pounds, or meet the girl/boy of your dreams. It's about loving yourself as you are right now. If you don't love yourself now, tomorrow won't be any different. You'll use the same excuses again to focus on everything you're not, and you'll repeat them throughout your lifetime. Today's the day to start appreciating everything God created you to be.

TO DO: Write down everything you love about yourself on sticky notes and paste them on your mirror. Then look at your reflection and read each one aloud over and over until you believe it.

TO PRAY: *Dear Lord, help me to be still and quiet so I can hear your gentle voice whispering, "You're terrific and special, my child!" Amen.*

MARCH 10 ▪ *Saturday of the Third Week*
HOSEA 6:1–6 » LUKE 18:9–14

Pharisee or tax collector?

Two men went to the temple to pray. Once was a Pharisee and the other was a tax collector. » LUKE 18:10

I've never forgotten the words Andrea said to her husband: "If I'm so bad, why did you marry me?" There's little that's more destructive and demeaning than a casual putdown, and her husband often used Andrea as the object of his degrading humor.

We've all experienced a backhanded compliment or sarcastic remark from a friend or family member. If we counter, we're accused of making a big deal out of nothing. But what *they* think is harmless humor takes an emotional toll on us, one putdown at a time. If you allow them to get to you, you begin to doubt yourself. You need to protect yourself. The tax collector can help.

As a recipient of the Pharisee's putdowns, the tax collector maintained his dignity. He didn't sink to the Pharisee's level or take it personally. Rather, he remained calm and prayed to God with confidence. This is the response we all need so that we don't end up being emotional wrecks.

If, however, you're like the Pharisee, you're delivering the putdowns of others so you can feel better about yourself. This is unacceptable. Just stop.

TO DO: Carry a small stone in your pocket. Whenever the urge comes to put people down, switch it to the other pocket to remind you not to do it.

TO PRAY: *Dear Lord, may my words lift people up and not bring them down. Amen.*

MARCH 11 ■ *Fourth Sunday of Lent*

2 CHRONICLES 36:14–16, 19–23 » EPHESIANS 2:4–10 » JOHN 3:14–21
OR, FOR YEAR A: 1 SAMUEL 16:1B, 6–7, 10–13A » EPHESIANS 5:8–14 » JOHN 9:1–41

Why me?

"Rabbi, who sinned, this man or his parents, that he was born blind?"
» JOHN 9:2

When life is ripped apart, we often ask, "Why me? What have I done to deserve this?" There are no answers to why bad things happen. Rather, the question should be: When bad things happen, what can you do? You can choose to withdraw from life, wallow in anger, and never move on, or you can turn your pain over to Jesus and welcome the new experience into your life.

A year ago, Kevin, a single father with two teenage children, was diagnosed with stage 2 lymphoma. He works full time and receives chemotherapy every couple of weeks. I asked him, "How do you get through each day with cancer?" Smiling, he said, "Every day is a miracle for me and I refuse to let anything or anyone ruin it, especially by being bitter or angry. I live for my kids and for today. Believe it or not, I'm happier now than I was before I was diagnosed."

Painful and unfair circumstances will happen. Go ahead and ask "Why?" but resist hanging on to that question. Let it go, like Kevin did.

TO DO: Do you know anyone going through a rough time? Call, write, or sit with them. Help them to become like Kevin.

TO PRAY: *Dear Lord, push me to reach out to a hurting friend. That may be the best medicine for them. Amen.*

MARCH 12 ■ *Monday of the Fourth Week*

ISAIAH 65:17–21 » JOHN 4:43–54

If they resist, persist

There was a royal official whose son was sick at Capernum.
» JOHN 4:46

"This can't be," Margaret screamed. "I just talked to him a couple of hours ago… he was on his way home." Margaret's son, Billy, had been killed by a drunk driver. "It has to be a nightmare," she said. "I'll wake up and we'll have breakfast."

Nothing is more devastating for a parent than when a child dies. I can't offer words of explanation for so great a loss. It's not supposed to happen this way. Dreams and plans are turned upside down. Parents expect their children to grow, play, dance, graduate, marry, and have children of their own. Throughout my ministry, I've sat with parents who have buried a son or daughter. I've found most never get over it. They just learn to live with the loss.

Rebuilding a new life without their child is life-changing. Suggest they join a support group and connect with other parents who understand what they're going through and who allow them to talk about their child. The pain won't disappear, but they'll walk away feeling understood, having found the right combination of support that works best for them.

TO DO: Grieving parents tend to isolate themselves when the crowd disappears. Check in on them. Take them to lunch, a movie, or your home. If they resist, persist.

TO PRAY: *Dear Lord, the death of a child leaves us speechless. Give me the courage to be a caring presence to those who are going through this unimaginable pain. Amen.*

MARCH 13 ■ *Tuesday of the Fourth Week*
EZEKIEL 47:1–9, 12 » JOHN 5:1–16

Slow down!

"When the water is stirred up, but while I am coming, another steps down before me."
» JOHN 5:7

We're dashing off to an appointment, wolfing down lunch while responding to emails, multitasking at mealtime, tucking the kids in, doing the laundry, and preparing for an important meeting. Whew. If this sounds all too familiar, you're suffering from rushing sickness. Side effects? Poor health and damaged relationships.

When we're always rushing against the clock, life rushes past us. We miss important moments in the lives of the people we love. Someday, we'll look back with regret. "I wish my teenager and I had taken that walk." "I wish I hadn't missed so many dinners with my spouse."

I'm calling for a revolution! Let's rebel against a hectic lifestyle. Join ARM—the Anti-Rushing Movement. Slow down. Stop burning the candle at both ends. Kick back and savor life's breathtaking moments—sunrises and sunsets, star gazing, seasons coming and going, a baby's first steps.

Join ARM, because one day, life will pass you by. Don't regret your choices. "I could have been with the family instead of working on the report." "I should have visited." Lily Tomlin nailed the remedy for rushing sickness: "For fast-acting relief, try slowing down." Things will get done anyway. You'll see.

TO DO: Richard Jolly suggested: When going on vacation, set up an email with this address: goaheadandruinmyvacation@....com. Any takers?

TO PRAY: *Dear Lord, you never rushed, but made time for every person. Help me follow your example and hop off this accelerating treadmill before I fall on my face. Amen.*

MARCH 14 ■ *Wednesday of the Fourth Week*

ISAIAH 49:8–15 » JOHN 5:17–30

The ultimate wake-up call

"For the hour is coming when all who are in their graves will hear his voice."
» JOHN 5:28

Short of breath, I was transported to the hospital. After my heart catheterization, the cardiologist told me my heart ejection fraction was well below normal. He referred me to a major heart hospital.

"Let's wait and see if the medication returns your heart muscles to normal," the doctor said. "Meanwhile, we'll put you on the transplant list."

"Transplant? That can't be!" I thought. Fortunately, after months of visits, the ejection fraction returned to normal.

Nothing prepares us for the possibility of death. At many funerals, I'd reminded people: "This could be your last day." Yet there I was waiting for death to knock on my door. We all live as though we have all the time in the world. But our next breath isn't guaranteed. This could be your last Wednesday.

My diagnosis was my ultimate wake-up call, recalibrating what's essential. Rather than taking life for granted, be grateful for this awesome gift and stop and smell the coffee. Soak in nature. Laugh often. Enjoy a child's smile. Converse with friends and family. I didn't want to die with unfinished business, having missed opportunities to express my love and forgiveness. The next time death knocks, I'm ready.

TO DO: Ask your family and friends what they'd do with only three months left to live.

TO PRAY: *Dear Lord, help me not to sleepwalk through life only to wake up realizing I wasted too much precious time. I want to live now, breath by breath. Amen.*

MARCH 15 ▪ *Thursday of the Fourth Week*
EXODUS 32:7–14 » JOHN 5:31–47

Meet me at the CAFÉ

"John was a burning light and shining light, and for a while you were content to rejoice in his light." » JOHN 5:35

Everybody has bad days, but does it seem like many people today are committed to complaining? We can't hide from them, especially if they're in our lives. When dealing with chronic complainers, try the CAFÉ approach.

Connect with them by validating their feelings. It shows you care about what they're saying.

Avoid offering solutions. Ask, "How are you going to handle this?" Listen to what they say.

Find a workable plan. Ask, "How will this fix the problem?" Then listen.

Execute. Do it. Tell them to put the plan in motion. Then check in with them to see how it's going.

Forget about cheering, solution-giving, or egging-on. Just understand and walk alongside them. Try the CAFÉ approach on your favorite complainer. The results might surprise you.

TO DO: For the remainder of Lent, commit to a "No Complaining" rule. If you don't like something, work to either change it or make peace with it.

TO PRAY: *Dear Lord, if I can't be positive, let me then be quiet. Amen.*

MARCH 16 ■ *Friday of the Fourth Week*
WISDOM 2:1A, 12–22 » JOHN 7:1–2, 10, 25–30

I'll get around to it

But when his brothers had gone up to the feast, then he himself also went up.
» JOHN 7:10

"Since I've had cancer," Alan told me, "when my wife or I say, 'Let's…,' the other says, 'Yes!'" Alan and his wife understand that there are so many possibilities and opportunities waiting to be seized and savored. Yet we often miss them because we wait for a more convenient time. We place people on the back burner, assuming they'll always be there.

It's called procrastination and many of us are masters of it. "I'll do it later," we say. Then tomorrow comes and we push it off again. Our self-talk convinces us there's plenty of time. Other things take precedence, and we get sidetracked by videos, blogs, or music.

The best way to avoid procrastination is to be deliberate in doing what you don't feel like doing. Tackle what's important. Get it done *now* by using different self-talk. "Okay, let's get moving and get this started." No excuses. You might need to bring a mentor on board who isn't afraid to confront and challenge you.

TO DO: What have you been putting off? Losing weight? Mending a relationship? Cleaning out closets? Job hunting? Write down the top three. Then ask (with a mentor): "How can I achieve my goal? What excuses do I have for waiting?" Now, do it.

TO PRAY: *Dear Lord, today I have my list of what I need to accomplish. Give me a little push and a lot of motivation so it's not still waiting for me tomorrow. Amen.*

MARCH 17 ■ *Saturday of the Fourth Week*

JEREMIAH 11:18–20 » JOHN 7:40–53

People needing people

"The Messiah will be of David's family and come from Bethlehem."
» JOHN 7:42

I love these words of Orson Welles: "Only through our love and friendship can we create the illusion for the moment that we're not alone." All of us are born with an unquenchable need for meaningful connections with others. It begins with our first breath and continues until we close our eyes for the last time.

Building relationships you desire—making them more intimate and more fun—helps to complete you as a person. We're all at our best plugged into working relationships with others; we're at our worst when we're unplugged. Without the feeling of connection, you can't develop into a complete person.

We all find ourselves face-to-face with people experiencing difficulties, frustrations, and pressures. They're in tears, feeling broken and defeated. Their lives are changed by circumstances, and they need someone to turn to.

Even though we're not therapists or counselors, we can offer support by showing up and seeing what they're going through—a breakup, betrayal, loss, depression, confusion. Help them get through by gently listening as they share their feelings and their plans. Then rejoice with them when they've made it through their heartache.

We all can comfort others with a small compliment, smile, dependable presence, kind act, listening ear, or warm touch.

TO DO: Find someone who's experiencing one of life's trials. Consider ways you can help without hurting.

FOR YOU TO SAY: *Dear Lord, I want to be able to lift up a friend when heartache knocks them down. Amen.*

MARCH 18 ■ *Fifth Sunday of Lent*

JEREMIAH 31:31–34 » HEBREWS 5:7–9 » JOHN 12:20–33
OR, FOR YEAR A: EZEKIEL 37:12–14 » ROMANS 8:8–11 » JOHN 11:1–45

When silence isn't golden

"Lord, if you had been here, my brother would never have died."
» JOHN 11:21

A man shared his unhappy life of troubles and failures with a priest. "There's a comedian in town. People leave the show hurting from laughter," the priest told him. "Treat yourself. Go to his show."

"Father," the man replied, "I *am* the comedian."

No one is meant to hurt alone. Yet many go through life with incredibly deep pain, choosing to suffer privately rather than step out and ask for help. After years of experience, I can sense when something is wrong, yet when asked, people tend to respond, "Everything's great!"

We've all encountered people in real pain. Some people retreat and conceal it. But others bravely step forward and reveal it, saying, "I need help."

Someone asking you for help is a compliment. They let you know they trust you in their vulnerability. They're not looking for answers or magic solutions. They just need someone who lets them know they're not alone.

Jesus connected with Martha's loss. She cried out and he listened, making her feel understood. Saying a healthy "I need you" is an important first step.

TO DO: Three words we need to hear: "I need help." Listen for them and respond quickly.

TO PRAY: *Dear Lord, help me recognize and respond to someone's cry for help. Amen.*

MARCH 19 ▪ *Saint Joseph*

2 SAMUEL 7:4–5A, 12–14A, 16 » ROMANS 4:13, 16–18, 22 » MATTHEW 1:16, 18–21, 24A
OR LUKE 2:41–51A

When friends are like family

Joseph her husband, being a righteous man and not wanting to disgrace her...
» MATTHEW 1:19

We've all said it. "When I was going through a tough time, I learned who my real friends were." Unfortunately, I've found times when life threw me curve balls and the friends I thought I could count on were nowhere to be found. Instead there were unexpected others who heard I was in need and showed up.

Cosmetic or consistent friends? Both are in our lives. Cosmetic friends live by the motto: "What's in it for me?" A successful woman accumulated friends who flocked around her, basking in her status and social networks, and benefiting financially. But when she lost her job, they abandoned her. Same for us: when our "value" is gone—poof! They disappear without a goodbye.

It's our consistent friends with whom we have a heart connection. They love us despite our shortcomings. Their loyalty strengthens with time. They stick with us through laughter, tears, good times, hardships, and difficulties, saying, "I have your back," and meaning it. When the crowds fade after a crisis, our consistent friends are still there, active, concerned, and involved. They drop everything at a moment's notice and come to help, asking, "What do you need?"

TO DO: Send a handwritten note to your consistent friends thanking them for the times they stuck by you. A few lines straight from your heart to let them know they're valued.

TO PRAY: *Dear Jesus, help me stick with my real friends, the way they stick with me. Amen.*

MARCH 20 — *Tuesday of the Fifth Week*
NUMBERS 21:4–9 » JOHN 8:21–30

Unfathomable pain

"Surely he will not kill himself, will he?" » JOHN 8:22

My friends' lives were changed in a split second. Cyberbullied by her so-called friends, their daughter was shamed by comments on social media aimed at ruining her reputation. On a Saturday afternoon in the fall of 2016, she took her own life. The letter she left behind spoke of desperation, helplessness, and worthlessness. She was profoundly depressed and wanted her pain to end.

What triggers such a tragic decision? For those left behind, the grief is heart-wrenching. Often besieged with guilt, they're haunted by questions: "Could I have prevented this?" "Why? Why?" They're tortured by "what if" and "if only" scenarios.

We can't know the pain residing in the hearts of others. Too often, they keep their loneliness, frustration, failure, and hopelessness well hidden. The only one with answers is the one who's gone.

If you have lost a loved one this way, take control of your journey from hurt to healing. You may never get over the tragedy, but you need to be at peace with its reality. Join a support group with people who understand your pain and have insights on how to cope because they've been there. Father William Byron wrote: "No one, therefore can judge a person whose choice we can't fathom, whose life we can remember, but can't restore, and whose pain we can't understand."

TO DO: If you are grieving over the suicide of a loved one, please pick up the phone and contact a suicide support group.

TO PRAY: *Dear Lord, help me to survive this loss. Give me courage to reach out for help. Amen.*

MARCH 21 ▪ *Wednesday of the Fifth Week*

DANIEL 3:14–20, 91–92, 95 » JOHN 8:31–42

Clearing out the clutter

"So, if a son frees you, then you will truly be free." » JOHN 8:36

We all have our list of persons who have hurt us. For some, the hurt comes from cruel words. For others, it's the discovery of their spouse's secret life. But whatever the cause, some people choose to live with the hurt instead of choosing to move toward healing.

When these people come to me, I sense their anger, resentment, and desire for revenge. After they vent, I ask, "Have you thought about forgiveness?" The response is usually the same: "Are you kidding me?"

We're in the home stretch of Lent, so it's an ideal time to clear out all the clutter of resentment in our hearts. Make the decision to sweep it out—every hurtful thing someone has said to you or about you, and all the ways they've wronged you. Get rid of it all. Forgive. Don't allow them to steal your peace and happiness.

Forgiveness is the permanent declutterer. It removes past hurts, relationship wounds, and nagging grudges. Open your heart to experience love and freedom from all those who've held you hostage. The key is forgiveness, and only you can open the door.

TO DO: Write the name of someone who's hurt you on one side of a card. On the other side, write the pain they caused. Get on your knees, hold these cards up to Jesus, ask him to help you forgive, and then, let it go.

TO PRAY: *Dear Lord, give me the courage to bury the pain, and the amnesia to forget about it. Amen.*

MARCH 22 ■ *Thursday of the Fifth Week*
GENESIS 17:3–9   »   JOHN 8:51–59

Taking the high road

So they picked up stones to throw at him, but Jesus hid and went out of the temple area. » JOHN 8:59

There's always someone who drives you crazy: your spouse's behavior gets under your skin, perhaps; a friend does all the talking, interrupts, and rarely listens; your parents push your buttons…

Most difficult people were slighted, wronged, ignored, or mocked sometime in their lives. Now they interpret everything through their pain and, in turn, they inflict their hurt and nastiness on us. It's up to us to steer clear of criticizing, belittling, or pointing out their faults to them—they know them already.

In order to manage difficult people, we need to take the high road and refuse their baiting. How we think, feel, and respond is wholly our responsibility. We must never relinquish that control to them. When we face off with them, we need to maintain our cool. Once the anger starts boiling inside you, take a deep breath and count to ten slowly. That way you can avoid escalating the issue and inflicting more pain.

TO DO: Choose your battles wisely. Difficult people who are stuck in their ways just aren't worth the emotional turmoil. They may refuse to change, but they don't have to change *you*. You're valuable, and so is your time. Don't waste it.

TO PRAY: *Dear Lord, I only have control over who I am and how I choose to act. When faced with people who are being difficult, give me the courage to walk away. Amen.*

MARCH 23 ■ *Friday of the Fifth Week*

JEREMIAH 20:10–13 » JOHN 10:31–42

Only if I let you!

Again they tried to seize him, but he escaped their grasp.
» JOHN 10:39

A monastery was attacked by warriors. Inside, they found an elderly monk who refused to surrender. Standing nose-to-nose with the monk, a warrior said, "If you don't surrender, I will run this sword through you." The monk replied, "Only if I let you."

Like the warrior set to destroy, some people walk around armed with critical spirits. They utter dreaded statements like, "Didn't I tell you so?" and "Truth be told; I warned you." They gloat. "You didn't believe me, but here we are." "See, I'm right and you're wrong. Again." Criticism and fault-finding seem to empower them as they confidently predict impending disaster.

Sometimes their words are dressed in disguises. "Didn't I tell you so?" is camouflaged as "See, it *was* a good idea to fix the faucet!" A surefire way to ward off the critics is to maintain the "only if I let you" attitude of the monk. Cover your ears, block out their words, and walk away. Give it a try. If you don't and you surrender to them, things will only get worse. You'll give them the power to make you feel guilty, incompetent, and inferior.

TO DO: *"Only if I let you."* Write it down. Carry it in your wallet. When you're attacked by critics, neutralize them with these words.

TO PRAY: *Dear Lord, give me the strength, determination, and persistence to stand up to the critics and claim my independence. Amen.*

MARCH 24 ■ *Saturday of the Fifth Week*

EZEKIEL 37:21–28 » JOHN 11:45–56

The choice is ours

"You do not realize that it is better for you that one man die for the people than that the whole nation perish." » JOHN 11:50

Ryan White was one of only 148 pediatric AIDS cases in the United States in 1984. Despite statements from doctors and the CDC that Ryan posed no risk to other children, fearful parents, teachers, and administrators petitioned the courts, unsuccessfully, to ban him from school.

They forced Ryan to eat with disposable utensils and plates and to use a separate bathroom. Kids vandalized his locker and called him names. After someone fired a bullet into their living room, Ryan's family moved to a new town and Ryan to a new school.

Sixteen-year-old Wendy Baker was on the student council there. Wendy went to Ryan's house and was the first to welcome him. She reached out and shook his hand.

Her simple act of compassionate kindness said to Ryan, "You have worth. We care about you." Wendy saw a person, not a disease.

The choices we make *do* matter. We can love someone for who they are, rather than for who we want them to be, building them up rather than tearing them down. We can treat them with respect and dignity instead of contempt and indignation. The choice is ours.

TO DO: Before you do something, ask yourself: Will it hurt anyone? Is it fair? Does it go against the Golden Rule? How will I feel about it later?

TO PRAY: *Dear Lord, the greatest privilege you've given me is choice. May I always choose wisely. Amen.*

MARCH 25 ◼ *Palm Sunday of the Passion of the Lord*

MARK 11:1–10 OR JOHN 12:12–16 » ISAIAH 50:4–7
PHILIPPIANS 2:6–11 » MARK 14:1—15:47

The ticking clock

But Peter said to Him, "Even though all may fall away, I will not."
» MARK 14:29

Matthew was taking his usual route home from work when his car collided with a tractor trailer. He was pronounced dead at the scene. My heart ached for his loved ones who experienced such a tragic, premature end to life.

Every day, we are reminded that life can change in a heartbeat. People's plans and dreams are interrupted unexpectedly due to accidents or illnesses. Every moment has value, and we should never let one pass by unnoticed.

Jesus can relate. Crowds lined the streets, welcoming and singing to their local boy who did good. Suddenly, however, everything changed. An associate sold him out for thirty coins. Those closest to him fell asleep at the time he most needed their support. His prized disciple, the "rock," the one who boasted of his loyalty, disowned him—not once, not twice, but three times.

Live in the moment. Tell your loved ones how much you treasure them. Appreciate all you have. If you're not happy with your life, make changes. It's never too late. Begin each day with these simple words: "Thank you, God!" He's given you a gift—a new day, a fresh start. Savor it. The clock is ticking.

TO DO: Stop procrastinating. Contact those you care about. This week, do something you've been putting off. Do it now!

TO PRAY: *Dear Lord, I know life doesn't stop and wait for anyone. Help me to live it moment by moment. Amen.*

MARCH 26 ■ *Monday of Holy Week*
ISAIAH 42:1–7 » JOHN 12:1–11

Come in and dine with me

But Judas Iscariot, one of his disciples, who was intending to betray him…
» JOHN 12:4

Compared to the rest of the disciples, Judas seemed trustworthy and had no obvious vices. He didn't have a dishonorable past like Matthew's, the tax collector turned disciple. He wasn't impulsive like Peter. He didn't have the temper of James and John.

So what motivated him? Greed? Envy? Who knows? What we do know is that regret drove him to take his own life. During those darkest moments, Judas must have felt "unforgivable"—like the most wicked scoundrel on Earth.

An African legend recounts the moment Judas died. Before passing from this world to the next, he walked down a dark road and saw a lit-up house. Approaching, he knocked on the door. Jesus opened it, embraced his friend, and invited him to dine with him.

It's a lifelong challenge to forgive people whom we feel don't deserve a second chance. Most of us write them off. But when we move toward forgiveness, we give the person who's harmed us an opportunity for healing. Imagine if Jesus withheld forgiveness as easily as we do. While the fact that Jesus forgives us doesn't give us license to deliberately mess up, it does give us the wisdom to learn from the mess-ups—and the strength to stop repeating them.

TO DO: Write "Just ask" on cards and pass them out to people who are having a hard time asking Jesus to forgive them.

TO PRAY: *Dear Lord, thank you for casting all my mess-ups into a lake and posting a "No Fishing Allowed" sign there. Amen.*

MARCH 27 ■ *Tuesday of Holy Week*

ISAIAH 49:1–6 » JOHN 13:21–33, 36–38

A gamble worth the risk

"Master, who is it?" After dipping the bread, Jesus handed it to Judas.
» JOHN 13:25–26

With three young children and promising careers, Barbara thought she had a great marriage. Then she read an email a woman sent to her husband: "Last night was one of the best evenings for me. I can't wait to see you again."

"I felt someone pulled the carpet right out from under my feet," Barbara told me. "I couldn't believe it."

Whether it's an unfaithful spouse, a disloyal friend, or a vindictive coworker, betrayal is painful, prompting feelings of resentment, anger, hurt, and disappointment, and it can take a long time to heal.

But Barbara wanted a relationship, not revenge. When her husband came home from work, she confronted him with what she knew, not holding back any of her feelings. Over the next few evenings, they discussed their marriage, what motivated the affair, and what was missing from their relationship. Then, together, they worked toward healing it. Barbara made it clear she wanted to trust him and not have to check his emails and texts. Eventually, they built a stronger marriage.

I've been told that rebuilding a relationship after a betrayal is one of life's biggest gambles. But in the end, it's worth risking. Through work and forgiveness, the present won't look at all like the past.

TO DO: If you've been betrayed, surround yourself with a support system. Connect with them often. Healing takes time, so don't rush it.

TO PRAY: *Dear Lord, you know how it feels to have someone turn on you. Help me to grow in trust again. Amen.*

MARCH 28 ■ *Wednesday of Holy Week*

ISAIAH 50:4–9A » MATTHEW 26:14–25

The blame game

"Surely, it is not I, Rabbi?" » MATTHEW 26:25

"He did that." "She said this." "It's not my fault." Sound familiar? The good old-fashioned blame game. Something goes wrong and it's your spouse, in-law, teacher, sibling, neighbor, etc., who is responsible. Surely it's "Not me!" We make excuses, dodge accountability, and point fingers—anything to redirect the spotlight to someone else. But blaming those closest to us when things go wrong can damage our relationships.

Shifting the blame can be time consuming. Rather than stepping up and accepting the consequences, we let it snowball. Before you discover that a situation is spiraling out of control, don't wait to see how it shakes out. When it's you who did wrong, own it.

The truth will eventually be revealed. But if you continually skirt the issue, you'll end up having egg on your face. Your credibility will be compromised, and you'll be terribly embarrassed. If you don't come clean with the boss, for example, your days at work may be numbered.

We all make mistakes. Confessing that you caused the problem and working to resolve it is how the game should be played.

TO DO: When you've made a mistake, stop and ask yourself: What caused the mistake? How can I avoid doing it again?

TO PRAY: *Dear Lord, when I point a finger of blame at someone else, help me to remember that there are three more pointing back at me. Help me to be accountable. Amen.*

MARCH 29 — *Holy Thursday*

EXODUS 12:1–8, 11–14 » 1 CORINTHIANS 11:23–26 » JOHN 13:1–15

Remember who you are!

"Do you realize what I have done to you?" » JOHN 13:12

Sometimes, on my frequent visits to Norman, he would know my name. Other times, he wouldn't. Eventually, he even forgot his own name. At the end, his body began to shut down. It's as if his lungs forgot to breathe and his heart forgot to beat. Alzheimer's is like that.

When Simba (*The Lion King*, 1994) runs with a different crowd, he loses his way. When he looks in the water, his reflection is the face of his father, Mufasa, reminding him, "Remember who you are." Teenagers often need that same reminder. So do we.

The moment we catch spiritual amnesia and forget our intrinsic God-given significance, we take a step backwards, opening ourselves up to all kinds of self-defeating behaviors. We say or do harmful things before realizing, "That's not who I am."

Today, remember you are a holy, unrepeatable masterpiece of God. You came into this world fully loaded and equipped—one of a kind, an original. Your uniqueness influences everything you do. Whatever challenges or difficulties life throws your way, know that you have the care and protection of the One who created you. Never forget that.

TO DO: Complete this sentence: "I am…" with only positive, life-affirming words. Remember this sentence whenever you feel down.

TO PRAY: *Dear Lord, sometimes I remember what I should forget—failures, struggles, or hurts caused by others. Help me not to dwell on them. Amen.*

MARCH 30 ▪ *Good Friday*

ISAIAH 52:13—53:12 » HEBREWS 4:14–16; 5:7–9 » JOHN 18:1—19:42

What will matter?

"It is finished." » JOHN 19:30

When someone says, "I have no regrets," I'm not sure I believe them. Haven't they spoken words they wish they hadn't, missed opportunities, or suffered losses? More often, I hear the opposite: "If I had a second chance to live my life over, I would do things so differently."

Once lived, each day is gone forever. If we could see just five minutes beyond death, we'd know how we should be living right now. A hundred years from now, it won't matter what our bank balance was, the kind of house we lived in, or the cars we owned. It's not going to matter if the laundry pile is high, the carpet is stained, the dishes are stacked, or the windows are smudged.

What will matter will be how we lived: the times we said, "I love you," "Thank you," or "Please forgive me"; the moments when life got the best of us and, rather than calling it quits, we called out to God. What will matter are the times we've seen broken people and responded with tenderness, compassion, and healing love.

So, if you did get another opportunity, what would you do differently?

TO DO: Be deliberate and pay attention to the people you love. Remember to listen, hug, and love while you still have the chance.

TO PRAY: *Dear Lord, every moment is an opportunity to be lived. Remind me to live now so I don't leave this world filled with regrets. Amen.*

MARCH 31 ■ *Holy Saturday (Easter Vigil)*

GENESIS 1:1—2:2 OR 1:1, 26-31A » GENESIS 22:1-18 OR 22:1-2, 9A, 10-13, 15-18
EXODUS 14:15—15:1 » ISAIAH 54:5-14 » ISAIAH 55:1-11 » BARUCH 3:9-15, 32—4:4
EZEKIEL 36:16-17A, 18-28 » ROMANS 6:3-11 » MARK 16:1-7

The empty egg

"He has been raised, he is not here." » MARK 16:6

Anthony, a first-grader with a brain tumor, was in Miss Hunt's class. The Friday before Easter, she gave each student a plastic egg. "Put a symbol of Easter inside. But don't put your name on it," she said.

On Monday morning, Miss Hunt's desk was filled with Easter eggs. A flower popped out of the first one. Alice said, "That's my egg!"

"What a wonderful symbol for Easter. Springtime. Everything coming to life," the teacher said.

The second egg was empty. *This must be Anthony's*, she thought, putting it aside.

"Miss Hunt," Anthony said, "that's my egg."

"But it's supposed to be a symbol for Easter," she said.

"I know," he explained. "The tomb was empty on Easter morning."

To be empty is to be full and complete. Hopefully, Lent has been a time for you to pour out all the harmful, negative ways of thinking that filled your head. Let the knowledge of how amazingly special you are pour over you and fill you. I hope you replaced any stockpiles of anger, guilt, and resentment with peace, happiness, and forgiveness. Most of all, may you count God *in* rather than counting God out, especially when darkness descends.

Anthony died after Easter. Miss Hunt's class placed Easter eggs near his casket. And all of them were empty.

TO DO: Try Miss Hunt's assignment and see what your family comes up with.

TO PRAY: *Dear Lord, help me to empty myself so I can be whole. Amen.*

ALSO BY JOSEPH SICA

"In this gentle gem, Father Joe admirably blends real-life stories, down-to-earth wisdom, and sparkling wit to make forgiveness as important and as necessary as breathing. This is, by far, the book to read for those who are struggling to move beyond their feelings of anger and revenge to forgiveness. It will change lives."

SISTER HELEN PREJEAN, *author of* **Dead Man Walking**

152 PAGES | $12.95 | 5½" x 8½" | 9781585957620

TO ORDER CALL 1-800-321-0411
OR VISIT WWW.TWENTYTHIRDPUBLICATIONS.COM

TWENTY-THIRD PUBLICATIONS
A division of Bayard, Inc.